The Iowa That Was

The Iowa That Was

*Memories of an Iowa Farm Boy
Turned Philosopher*

Wayne Gustave Johnson

RESOURCE *Publications* • Eugene, Oregon

THE IOWA THAT WAS
Memories of an Iowa Farm Boy Turned Philosopher

Copyright © 2022 Wayne Gustave Johnson. All rights reserved. Except for brief quotations in critical publications or reviews, no part of this book may be reproduced in any manner without prior written permission from the publisher. Write: Permissions, Wipf and Stock Publishers, 199 W. 8th Ave., Suite 3, Eugene, OR 97401.

Resource Publications
An Imprint of Wipf and Stock Publishers
199 W. 8th Ave., Suite 3
Eugene, OR 97401

www.wipfandstock.com

PAPERBACK ISBN: 978-1-6667-3634-2
HARDCOVER ISBN: 978-1-6667-9449-6
EBOOK ISBN: 978-1-6667-9450-2

JUNE 20, 2022 9:47 AM

In Memory of

Dad and Mom

Johan Gustaf Johannesson

Ruth Helen Victoria Hanson Johnson

Contents

Illustrations | viii

Acknowledgements | ix

1	Swedish Roots	1
2	Odebolt, Iowa, My Home Town	5
3	The Farm	10
4	Country School	19
5	The Little Church that Nurtured Me	31
6	Labor Intensive Farming	35
7	Horsepower on the Farm	41
8	The Farmer's Wife: My Mom	44
9	How We Ate	48
10	Trapping, Hunting, and Fishing	53
11	Sex Education on the Farm	60
12	Our Values	64
13	My Dad Dies	70
14	In Retrospect	76

Illustrations

Johannesson brothers | 27
Odebolt, Iowa, Main Street | 28
Model T Truck and children | 29
Clinton No. 3 Country School | 30

Acknowledgements

Photos by the courtesy of The Chronicle and Odebolt History Pages

1

Swedish Roots

IN THE LATE NINETEENTH CENTURY, the Småland Province of Sweden was a good place to be *from*. Although surrounded by provinces noted for productive farmland, Småland was marked by rocky ground, woods, and streams. Winters were bitter cold. At least they had snow for skiing, ice for skating, and rocks for kurling. Legend has it that while God was creating the neighboring provinces of Sweden, Satan sneaked ahead and created Småland. The only thing that the Lord could do was to create a people—tough and determined—who could cope in that setting. Give Smålanders a rock and they could make it into a garden. My father was born in Småland on September 5, 1887.

The nineteenth century brought about major changes. Sweden had lost control of northern territories to Russia, under Peter the Great, in the early 1700s. Following a history of various other wars, Sweden has been at peace since 1814. Immigration to the United States from Sweden swelled during the latter half of the nineteenth century. Between 1851 and 1930, some 1,500,000 Swedes immigrated to the United States. A major cause of early immigration was the famine of 1867 to 1869, which was brought about by a year of extreme cold and then a year of drought. Both natural disasters severely diminished the food supply for human beings and for livestock. The industrial revolution gradually entered Sweden and helped to raise the economy of the nation and its peoples by the late nineteenth century.

My father, Johan Gustaf Johannesson, was born in Småland when the area was plagued with extreme poverty. His parents lived on a small farm called Björkelund or "place of many birches." Eleven children were born to his parents, Johannes and Hilda Jonasson. Five of these eleven survived. Two daughters, Emma and Anna, remained in Sweden, while three sons, Karl, Johan, and Ernst, all eventually immigrated to the United States. Hilda, the mother, died in 1895 at 39 years of age, after giving birth to stillborn triplets. The father, Johannes, died in 1901 at 51 years of age. My father, Johan Gustaf, was thirteen when his father died. I was also thirteen when my father died.

The State Church of Sweden

The Lutheran Church of Sweden served as the social service agency that cared for orphan children. Even though my father was only 13, he was deemed old enough to work for himself. He was placed on a farm where he was basically a farmhand, almost a slave. Family history indicates that the farmer who took my father in was stingy, harsh, and spanked my father regularly. My father had to sleep in a barn where livestock were kept, and there he shared fleas with the farm animals. The fleas were so bad that his neck became raw. In desperation, my 13-year-old father fled from the farm to his older sister's place of residence. He stayed with his sister and her future husband where he worked for him and his brother on alternating weeks.

Evidently Karl, Johan, and Ernst attended school for a few years. They walked some 11 miles to the school, through woods and streams. My father, Johan, had some four or five years of school. This was probably true of Karl and Ernst as well. Karl was evidently known as a bright student.

Swedish Roots

My father and his two brothers joined the wave of immigrants who came from Sweden around the turn of the century. Karl arrived in Boston in 1901 at sixteen years of age, six months after his father died. A friend in Pipestone, Minnesota, had funded his trip from Sweden as a steerage passenger, the lowest location in the ship's hold. Oral tradition has it that the ticket was sent to the State Lutheran Church in Sweden from the Lutheran Church in Pipestone. Karl had $5 in his pocket when arriving in Boston; he then made his way to Pipestone. A story relates that when Karl arrived by train in Pipestone, he saw some fair-haired girls near the station. They happened to be Norwegian but knew enough Swedish to help him make contact with his friend. Karl worked for his friend for three years to pay for the passage fare of $300. Apparently, Karl eventually decided that he had fully financed his passage to the United States so he left Pipestone and began farming for himself in Iowa.

My father, Johan Gustaf Johannesson, at 16 years of age, arrived in Boston by way of Liverpool, England, in 1904. Brother Karl paid for his passage. From Boston, my father made his way to Pipestone, Minnesota, to join his brother, Karl. Ernst, the youngest brother, arrived in New York City in 1910 with passage paid for by brothers Karl and Johan. He was nineteen years of age.

The three brothers eventually married and began farming near Odebolt, Iowa. Two wives were Swedish immigrants; the third—Johan's wife, my mother—was a daughter of Swedish immigrants. I have not checked my DNA, but my genes must be largely Swedish, although Norwegian and Finns have provided other genes for some who thought they were 100% Swedes..

Mother was born on February 14, 1898, near Odebolt, Iowa. Her parents, Eric Hanson and Hedvig (Hattie) Anderson, were both born in Sweden and immigrated to the States. My mother had two brothers, both of whom served in WWI, and four sisters. My mother graduated from the eighth grade, and then went to work on the farm her parents rented. Oral tradition has it that my father and mother first met when they were both picking corn at a Noyd farm near Odebolt. Dad and Mom married on March 15, 1920, in Sioux City, Iowa.

In the 1940 census, my father was listed as Gust Johnson. There are no records that clarify why the name was altered. It may have been changed to avoid confusion since there were, no doubt, many John Johnsons. Johan Gustaf Johannesson—now "Gust J. Johnson"—and his wife, Ruth Helen Victoria Hanson, settled on a farm near Odebolt. Five Johnson children were born on that farm: Howard, Helen, Virginia, Elaine, and Wayne. After I was born in 1930, Gust and Ruth evidently decided that five children were enough—perhaps too many!

2

Odebolt, Iowa, My Home Town

WHEN THE FIRST SUCCESSFUL English colony was established at Jamestown, Virginia, in 1607, some 30,000 Algonquian Indians lived in the region. As colonization expanded, many eastern Indian tribes were forced west and moved into the territory that was to become Iowa where they joined other tribes already in the region. By that time, the indigenous tribes no doubt looked upon the Europeans as a type of invasive species. When Iowa became a state in 1846, most Indian peoples were either driven out or bought out by European immigrants. Half a century later, my parents became part of that wave of immigrants.

In 1872 the Chicago and Northwestern Railroad reached into western Iowa. The coming of the railroad helped to plant a small town along a creek. The town took on the name of the creek which ran through it—the Odebolt Creek. The precise origin of the name Odebolt has never been definitively confirmed. Several legends have grown up about the name's origin. The most likely story has it that a Frenchman by the name of Jacques Odebeau trapped along that creek. The creek became known as Odebeau's Creek but was evidently corrupted into "Odebolt." Whatever the etymology may be, the little town grew to as many as 1,400 citizens at one point in its history. Since farms are now larger and farm families smaller, the town has lost population. It now boasts a bit below 1,000 local Odeboltians. Odebolt, Iowa, is my home town.

Odebolt takes up about one square mile of flat, fertile Iowa farmland. Its main role in history has been that of furnishing developing farms and farm families whatever was needed for farming operations and farm families. Businesses and churches developed. A local citizen took special interest in growing popcorn. When a Chicago company needed an adequate source of popcorn for its venture into the sale of sugared popcorn varieties, it bought the popcorn plant already established in Odebolt. That company became known as Cracker Jack, and Odebolt was proclaimed to be the Popcorn Center of the World. While Cracker Jack no longer does business in Odebolt, I do not know of any city that has tried to wrest that title from my home town. It may be that Sac City, a neighbor of Odebolt, could claim the title, since in 2016, the World's Largest Popcorn Ball was made there. Weighing 9,370 pounds, the popcorn ball is on display in Sac City. Visitors are welcome. Some consumer groups consider Cracker Jack to be the first junk food to be marketed.

Adams Ranch

Odebolt has a neighbor on its near south side that has a remarkable history of its own. The neighbor, known as Fairview Farms or the Adams Ranch, was created in 1890 when William P. Adams bought ten square miles of fertile farm land at that location. W. P. Adams had his own immigrant roots, tracing his family back to John Adams and John Quincy Adams, both Presidents of the United States. W.P. Adams bought the land after farming for a few years in North Dakota and then spent some years in business in Chicago. Apparently, he had an urge to get back into farming.

A businessman farmer, Adams ran a highly organized and integrated farming operation. Since this was long before tractors and other machinery were on the scene, the farm was operated with the help of some 240 mules brought up from Missouri. During the busy season, 150 men were employed with 45 kept on during the slack season. The mules were harnessed to plows, discs, rakes, planters, and wagons of various kinds. During summer months, dozens of mule teams pulling cultivators could be seen weeding corn rows that were one mile long. Other square-mile fields were completely sown to oats. For an operation of this size, a cluster of buildings was needed. Among these were a bunk house for the men with a kitchen and dining hall, a huge barn for the mules, grain bins for crops, and machine sheds to house and store various farming implements. There were also several homes for workers with families and, of course, a lovely house for the Adams family. The family also owned several smaller farms in the area which were rented out to farmers. I grew up on one of those tenant farms.

The farm on which I grew up was some seven miles from Odebolt. Four of those miles were gravel while three were paved with concrete. The town was the main source for groceries, hardware, and various supplies and equipment needed for farming. During my childhood years, the town had three grocery stores, three automobile dealerships, and two tractor companies. Two of the grocery stores also sold clothing and other household needs. Moreover, Odebolt boasted a hotel, a pool hall, a coffee house, a drug store, one restaurant, and a movie theatre—the Princess Theatre. Among professionals, there were three doctors, one lawyer, and one banking operation.

During the years I attended high school, Odebolt had one large school building from grades one through eight, and a newer high school building. While my high school years move beyond the story in this book, I do recall being surprised when I learned that the University of Wisconsin fight song was evidently plagiarized from Odebolt's.

Odebolt: Business and Social

During the spring through fall months, farm families would come into town to do the needed shopping. These visits also had a social dimension since it gave farm families an opportunity to chat with neighbors. One gathering place for farmers was a bench of some forty-feet in length. It was built off the sidewalk in a place where a burned-out building had not been replaced. Sometimes referred to as the "bull pen," farm wives and other women often felt self-conscious when they had to walk by that row of men on the bench. I do not, however, recall that any unruly behavior was ever demonstrated by the seated males. No whistling or hooting. One particularly nervy farmer's wife would walk right up to the men on the bench and "shoot the breeze" with them. I should add that this woman was not my mother.

During the summer months, the Odebolt High School band would perform a concert in Monument Circle just off of Main Street. Our family would come into town on most Saturday evenings for shopping and also on Wednesday evenings during the main summer months. Most of the time, all seven of us crowded into our 1932 Oldsmobile for the trip. Dad would bring various farm produce to sell to local dealers—chickens, eggs, and cream. This income helped purchase needed groceries.

My favorite locations in Odebolt on those shopping visits were the Watts Drug Store and Charlie Nelson's Variety Store. The drug store had a soda fountain where I would occasionally get an ice cream cone or, on a good night, a malted milk. Charlie Nelson's Variety Store had a display of candy, gum, and other goodies. Mr. Nelson would stand patiently while we farm children, clutching our nickel or dime, would carefully make our purchase. Those were the days when a five-cent Baby Ruth candy bar was quite large.

During my younger days, I would always stay with my dad when we were in town shopping and carefully follow him around. One Saturday evening, my mother caught me following the wrong man around downtown Odebolt. Evidently I registered some complaint when my mother intercepted me, but I saw the wisdom of her action when told that the man I was following was not my dad.

Odebolt, Iowa, My Home Town

Getting Lost in Odebolt

One rather odd—and somewhat embarrassing—memory was that of getting "lost" in downtown Odebolt one Saturday night. I note that it was somewhat embarrassing because there are only three or four blocks of stores and buildings that made up downtown Odebolt. In retrospect, it seems difficult to imagine how one could actually get lost in that setting. Nevertheless, I did. We had parked our car in a lot behind one of the stores, and I was old enough to wander off on my own for part of the evening. When I decided that it was time to return to the family car, I realized that I had lost my bearings. If not actually frightened, I did become nervous. As a rather shy lad, I would have hesitated to ask any passerby for help. I also knew that if I could locate Charlie Nelson's Variety Store, I could regain my bearings and find my way to the parked car. Finally I succeeded. The 1932 Oldsmobile never looked as good as it did when I found it that evening. Embarrassed by the episode, I didn't tell anyone that I had been lost.

When my father died in 1944, we moved into town. Odebolt remained my resident location until I attended Iowa State College in the fall of l949. The cozy and friendly little town became my home base for years to come.

3

The Farm

"You can take the boy off of the farm,
but you can't take the farm out of the boy."
—IOWA FOLK WISDOM

Much of the flat farmland of Iowa is criss crossed with gravel roads east-west and north-south at one mile apart. This creates many one square mile tracts of farmland of 640 acres. These square-mile parcels were usually divided into quarters, creating four distinct farms of 160 acres each. Before tractors came on the scene, a farm of 160 acres was about the size limit for one farmer to handle with horses and a hired man on occasion. My life began on one of those quarter-section farms.

My mother once declared that you could get the boy off of the farm, but you could never get the farm out of the boy. The stories I am now writing reflect some truth in that wisdom. This may also be reflected in a quip an Iowa State Singers coed once offered. Our Singers group was on a bus heading for our next concert. There was always a good deal of conversation and humor shared on those long trips. I do not recall the specific content of the conversation that went on that time, but Alice Lawrence, a soprano from Chicago, turned to me and observed, "Wayne, you're so rural."

My early years as a farm boy are also reflected in my sensitivity toward weather, which stays with me to this day. To farm is to gamble that nature will be helpful. This is not always the case. In my early years, especially the summer of 1936, we experienced devastating droughts. Anxiety grew in all of our family as the days and weeks went by without much rain, and the crops withered in the fields. My parents did not talk much about the drought. They tended to be stoic about the matter, but we, as children, were aware of the feelings. That feeling of anxiety is still deep within me and is aroused when there is need of rain wherever I live. My letters and emails to my children almost always include some comment about the weather we are experiencing. I may be off the farm, but the farm is still in me.

Dad Rented the Farm

Dad was never in a financial situation that allowed him to try to buy a farm of his own. One loss came when his younger brother, Ernst, died in his late twenties. Ernst had a wife, one child, and another on the way when he died. This was not only a personal loss for Dad, it was also a financial loss since he was sharing the farming with his brother. After Ernst's death, his widow, needing income, kept house for a bachelor neighbor, Mr. Norlin, for a few years. They eventually married, and Mr. Norlin adopted the two sons. He turned out to be a very fine father. One of the boys was killed in WWII—a sad memory.

Dad rented the farm from a very rich family who owned a number of other farms in the area and also ran the Adams Ranch—ten square miles of the finest farm land in Iowa. That large ranch was farmed with the help of itinerant laborers who came every summer season to drive the mules up and down the rows of corn. That was before tractors came onto the scene. During WWII, German prisoners of war were brought to the farm to replace Americans who had been drafted. I recall that grain wagons, pulled by mules and driven by German POWs, came down the road just a block from our home. U.S. sentries stood guard at various points along the route. My guess is that those POWs felt they were better off as mule drivers in the States rather than face the disasters of the German army near the end of that war. The Germans had good reputations as workers; not so the Italians who were also there for a while. Rumor had it that the Italians were apt to quit their work and chase a rabbit if one showed up in the field. An ethnic slur? Probably. I do not recall that our little town and rural community had any Italians as residents. Our neighbors were mostly Germans, Swedes, and a few Irish.

Iowa Share Cropping

Dad rented the farm on a "share crop" basis. This was basically the same arrangement that faced the freed slaves after the Civil War. These freed men had no means to buy a farm, so some ended up farming the land that their former slave owners still owned. For Dad, this share cropping meant that the owners of the farm received a certain percentage—I think it was fifty percent—of the grain crops each year. Dad could have rented for "cash," but if crops were bad any year he would still have to pay all the rent. So "share cropping" was a safer arrangement. We shared the abundance with the owners in good years as well as the meager results during years of drought or hail storms.

When I taught about Marxism years later, I would use Dad's rental arrangement as an example of what Marx called "exploitation." (Marx used the term in a technical sense, not as a moral judgment since Marx thought that capitalists were, themselves, victims of an historical economic process.) The owners of the land profited from my parents' labor even though the owners did no labor of their own to add to the value of the crops. The owners hired others to run the farmer's rental arrangements. Exploitation it may have been, but Dad seemed pleased to be able to make a living for his family in his adopted country. It was a better life than he would have known in Sweden. Our income level was probably on the edge of poverty, but we always had a place to live, food to eat, clothes to wear, and a happy family to enjoy.

Since most of our farm neighbors and friends were not wealthy, I do not have any recollection of actually feeling "poor." On the other hand, there was a clear distinction between our economic status and the wealth of the owners of the farm we rented. This was vividly expressed one Christmas season when a member of the family that owned our farm came to our farm home in a dark green chauffer-driven Cadillac limousine. The family member did not get out of the Cadillac. Instead, we farm kids went out to meet them. We each received Christmas presents from the passenger in the auto. My present was a very nice pencil box filled with a variety of drawing and writing devices. It was, no doubt, the best pencil box in Clinton No. 3 Country School.

The First Farm Home

I was born on a farm near Odebolt, Iowa, but we moved to another farm when I was four years of age. I have few memories of that first farm home, although I remember one incident with our generally good-natured family dog, Teddy. I was probably about three at the time. Teddy bit me when I patted his tummy too vigorously. Teddy intended it as a warning. No damage was done, but it was a memorable occasion for me.

In March, 1935, we moved from that farm largely because of an inadequate water supply. In dry weather, the well and the windmill failed to supply enough water for our livestock. Dad had to go to a neighbor's place with a large water tank to bring home the needed water. The farm we moved to had a well and windmill located in a creek-bed. Even in the driest years, like the summer of 1936, we never ran out of water. The well and windmill were located half a mile from what we called the "supply tank" near our house and the farm buildings. The windmill would pump water from that well through a line of underground pipes into that supply tank. The tank was high enough to supply sufficient water pressure to reach various places for the cattle and hogs and our porch.

During cold winter days, my dad would hang a lighted kerosene lantern in the lower supply tank structure to keep the water lines from freezing.

The Farm House I Remember

The house was a hybrid. One part of the house was built at one time and a larger addition attached later. The older section included one large room—which was our kitchen—two smaller rooms and an upstairs room reached by stairs. The addition included a dining room, a living room, two bedrooms, and a pantry on the first floor. There were four bedrooms upstairs which could be reached by two sets of stairs, one on both ends of the bedroom units. My siblings and I often chased each other up one set of stairs, through the bedrooms, and down the other set of stairs.

Before Electricity

There was no electricity on the farm when we moved onto it. The main sources of light in the evenings were two types of lamps. One was made with a simple wick that brought the kerosene up to the flame at the top of the wick which was inside a glass chimney. Another and brighter lamp also had the kerosene and wick, but the flame created a warm bright glow from a fragile mantel which enclosed the flame on the wick. This gave enough light so that Dad could read the paper as he sat near it. Dad also had a classic farm kerosene lantern that he used around the farm when he needed light. I do not recall that we ever used candles as a source of light, although we did put small wax candles on our Christmas tree every year. This was done with care since the pine trees could go up in flames very easily.

The Farm

Radio for News and Entertainment

Even without electricity, we did have a radio that was powered by an automobile battery. A long wire strung out from the front porch served as an antenna. Each year a pair of barn swallows would build a nest under our front-porch eave. While Mrs. Swallow would be laying and incubating the eggs, Mr. Swallow would sing his proud little heart out as he perched on the antenna. A fond memory. We listened regularly to the "Iowa Barn Dance Frolic" out of WHO, a Des Moines, Iowa, radio station. I think that was the only station we could receive. As children we had some favorite mystery shows on the radio that fed our imaginations: "I Love a Mystery," "Jack Armstrong," and a few others. All this, of course, was long before television.

Joe Louis was a favorite of Dad and of those of us who liked boxing. We could not see the action, of course, but the broadcaster always kept our interest. I recall Dad's pleasure when Joe Louis, the "Brown Bomber," knocked out Max Schmeling (Maximillian Adolph Otto Siegfried *Schmeling*) in the first round of their world championship heavyweight rematch in 1938. Schmeling had defeated Louis in a bout some two years earlier. The second fight had a certain nationalist flavor to it, given the rise of the Nazis in Germany. Hitler took an element of pride in Schmeling. Most Americans were pleased to see the German defeated. Dad certainly did. According to a childhood memory by President Jimmy Carter, Afro-Americans near his home celebrated enthusiastically. Fondness for Joe Louis may have helped pave the way for Blacks to get into other professional sports.

The Coming of Electricity

In the late 1930s, thanks to the Rural Electrification Administration, electricity was brought to the farm. The house and the barn were the only buildings wired. There was also a large pole near the center of farm buildings that held a yard light. The light fixtures in the house were cheap. The main ceiling light in the living room was a fixture for two light bulbs and no shade or chandelier—good enough for tenant farmers. But light was there, and we thoroughly enjoyed the modern convenience. We soon bought an electric toaster that did one piece of bread at time. We also purchased an electric coffee percolator. Dad installed an electric motor on Mom's washing machine, which had been run by a little Briggs and Stratton gasoline engine. It made washing day much quieter.

When we moved into town in 1944, we brought that little Briggs and Stratton engine into town with us. I first mounted it on our push lawnmower, then on my bicycle. I reversed the gearing on the lawnmower so that the blades ran the wheels instead of the other way around. Both experiments were moderately successful in operation, although the bicycle ran a little too fast since I had it rigged for only one wooden pulley that was wired to the rear-wheel spokes. It's a wonder that I managed to survive all those early inventions.

No Running Water

On our farm, we did not have running water in our house. Instead, on a concrete porch off the kitchen, there was a faucet where we drew the water we needed from the supply tank. The only plumbing we had in the house was a drain in the kitchen sink, which ran out to an open cesspool in a grove some distance from the house. There was no bathroom in the house. The outhouse served for basic needs. For our baths, we heated water on the kitchen stove in a large copper boiler. The stove was heated by various fuels—corn cobs, wood, or coal. I bathed once a week—probably at most—in a round galvanized tub placed in the kitchen for that occasion. That tub and bath water were shared with my siblings. We all bathed in the same tub and probably the same water, although more hot water was added when the late bathers had their turn in the tub. I do not recall my position in the line-up for bathing. Even bathing was labor intensive on the farm.

The Farm

The Famous Farm Outhouses

Since there was no bathroom in the house, toilet requirements were met by what would often be called "outhouses." Ours was about forty feet from the back door of the kitchen. It was a small building, about six feet by five inside, and about seven feet from floor to ceiling with no windows, just the front wooden door. It was built over a pit that served as sewage disposal plant. There were three levels inside the little building. One was the floor with two higher ones for sitting. Some old farm outhouses had only one hole. Ours was advanced—it had three holes. Two larger holes on a wooden bench were at the highest level. On a slightly lower level, there was a smaller hole for children. Toilet paper was never purchased. The Sears Roebuck and Montgomery Ward catalogues served the purpose, although the glossy pages were avoided..

A variety of stories can be told about these farm outhouses. Halloween tricksters—usually young males in the area—were known to upset these outhouses as a prank. One account has it that one farmer decided to sit inside his outhouse with a shotgun to frighten off such pranksters. The pranksters, however, were aware of his plans, so they sneaked up behind the outhouse and pushed if over onto its only door.

This, evidently, meant that the farmer's only escape route was through the toilet holes.

I do not remember that our outhouse was ever overturned. There were years when pranksters would upset the outhouses that were on the grounds of the country schools. One year, when dad was supervisor for the school, he bolted 2″ x 10″ planks to these outhouses and then to an adjoining building that held coal for the school house furnace. Problem solved.

Other Farm Buildings

Our barn was the most impressive building on our farm. In Iowa, ordinary farmers often took pride in the barns they displayed, not so much in their houses. Wealthier farmers would have houses of some beauty. Our barn was a two-story building. The top story was for storing hay and straw while the first floor was made up of a variety of stanchions for horses and others for milk cows. It also had a large feeding room for cattle during winter. The barn had a rail and manure-bucket mechanism which saved work. We would pitch the manure from the cattle or horse stanchions into the "bucket" (too large to be called a bucket), and then pull it down a rail to the outside of the barn where the manure could be dumped.

While we lived on that farm, both the corncrib and the hog house were replaced with new buildings. A new outhouse and a storage building were also built. The new corncrib had a concrete floor between two cribs and functioned as a garage for our car.

Our farm buildings also included a chicken house, corncrib, hog house, and a machine shed where harvesting equipment was stored. We also had a small building near the house where Mom did the laundry before electricity and where corncobs and coal were stored.

4

Country School

"In the little red school house, with my book and slate. In the little red school house, where I was always late."

—WILSON AND BRENNAN

My country schoolhouse was neither the fabled one-room country school nor was it the little red school house. Iowa had invested a good deal of money in making many well-built school houses of more than one room. All were painted white. The school I attended had one large classroom, but there was also one small room where we hung our coats and left our overshoes and where we had drinking water. There was another small room that was used for storage and also functioned as a workshop where we made various small furniture items out of three-ply wooden sheets. My mother would find some place to use the little items that I made at school—more out of loyalty to her son than of admiration for what he produced. I still remember that some of the brads I used to secure a shelf to the sides of a corner knick-knack shelf went astray and stuck out of the shelf. Mom used it anyway.

The large classroom contained rows of chairs of various sizes. Each chair had a steel frame and a study desk on top made of nicely finished wood. There was a storage area under the desk top that was used for books and writing equipment. There was also an ink well on each desk top, but I do not recall ever using ink or an ink pen. It may be that available ink had become too much of a temptation and a behavior problem. (The song, "The Little Red Schoolhouse," suggests just such a problem.) We wrote with lead pencils, not fountain pens. Ball point pens were invented some years later.

A large furnace stood in the corner of the large room. We would crowd around that furnace in the early hours of cold winter days until the room warmed up. Some twenty yards from the school house stood girls' and boys' "outhouses," which were erected over holes in the ground. The seats were made of lumber about one and one-half inches thick. The holes were sawed through that lumber at an angle. I am quite certain that these toilets were not equipped with regular toilet paper. In place of that luxury, we probably had a supply of either Montgomery Ward or Sears Roebuck catalogs. We were used to such resources since these were the same paper used at home in our outhouses. The school yard contained a rather nice set of two swings and a trapeze bar on a tubular steel frame. The school yard was large enough to allow us space to play softball.

The Johnsons Open Clinton No. 3

Clinton No. 3 had not been open the year before our family moved near to that school. There were not enough children in the area to warrant hiring a teacher and running the school. On March 1, 1935, our family moved to a farm that was close to that school. After the move, my four siblings finished that school year by becoming part of a rural school some two miles away. In the fall of 1935, Clinton No. 3 was opened for the four Johnsons (Howard, Helen, Virginia, Elaine) and a few neighborhood children. I began school there at five years of age in the fall of l936 when my three sisters were still in that school.

Howard graduated from the eighth grade in the spring of 1936 and began high school in Odebolt that fall. He either walked or rode his bicycle some two miles of gravel road to a neighbor's farm and rode with that family to Odebolt High School, another six miles away. Helen joined in that ride with Howard when she began high school in 1937. Dad and Mom paid the neighbor for this transportation help.

Our Teachers

In those days, country-school teachers started teaching in country schools right after high school where they had some initial teacher training. One of my sisters started teaching in one of those schools when she was only sixteen years of age. Most of these teachers did not look upon teaching as a lifelong vocation. Instead, they usually ended up marrying a young farmer in the area. My three sisters reflected this pattern. All three taught country school after high school for a few years before they married.

I look back on all of my teachers as kind young women and good teachers. There was one exception. This was an older woman who was, I think, unhappy about her life situation. She was very stern and set the tone on the first day of school by slapping a fellow classmate in the face for what seemed to me to be a rather trivial incident. I do not recall that she ever slapped any student after that day. The tone had been set. I never had any trouble with this teacher, but my sister Elaine would have to go home feeling ill some days since she was so terrified by the teacher. That teacher's contract was not renewed the next year.

Our teacher also functioned as custodian and janitor. She would bring water to the school everyday since there was no water source at the school itself. (I use the feminine pronoun for our teachers. It would have been unheard of for a man to teach a country school.) We must have had a place to wash our hands, but I do not recall that. The teacher would also have to sweep the floor. In the wintertime she would arrive early to bring coal in from the coal house some twenty yards away and start the fire in the furnace before the children arrived.

Some accounts of rural Iowa schools tell of large teen-age farm boys who were discipline problems for a young teacher right out of high school. This was not generally a problem in the country school I attended. I was among the teenage boys by the time I was in the upper grades, and my closest boy classmates were well behaved. There was one exception. He was living with his sister and her husband on a nearby farm. I do not recall his connection—if any—with his parents. He was probably four years older than the rest of us boys and showed signs of bullying on occasion. Only on rare occasions was he a behavior problem for the teacher.

A Stand for Justice

I do recall one incident with that boy that makes me proud of my sister, Elaine. The boy had picked up a switch and was bullying two smaller boys of the same family who had recently enrolled in our school. I must confess that I stood by with a sense of disapproval but without the courage to intervene in any way. The boy was much larger than I. But Elaine intervened. She grabbed the switch from him and broke it over her knee. The boy was surprised by the act and also a bit confused. He realized that he should not attack a girl for her actions—a norm for those days. As I recall, the entire incident settled down. I still admire persons who are willing to stand up for what they believe to be just and right.

The Three Rs

The curriculum was basically reading, writing, and arithmetic. While one class—or student—was meeting with the teacher, the rest of us would work on our assignments or eavesdrop—or day dream. There was a waist-level sandbox in the large room, and when I finished with my assigned work, I was allowed to play in that sandbox. This helped to keep me from being bored.

I do not remember any of my teachers treating me unjustly or unfairly. I do, however, recall an incident when I felt as though I had been tricked by a teacher. This teacher was the mother of our regular teacher and was substituting one day. I was in the first grade and was learning to carry in subtraction. She would put the problems on the chalkboard and I would work my way through them. All was going nicely until the teacher began to mark every other problem wrong on a new set of problems I had just finished. This was especially embarrassing since every student in that school room could see that I had erred. As it turned out, the problems marked wrong were problems that did not involve carrying; but I carried anyway. My five-year-old ego was badly punctured since I believed I was pretty good at arithmetic. In retrospect, it was a learning experience. My ego recovered.

Country School Arts

Our music lessons were limited. While there was a small pump organ in the large room, I do not recall that any of my teachers could play the instrument. Certainly none of the farm children took piano lessons. We did have a wind-up Victrola record player at the school. It had a picture of a dog listening to a speaker with the caption "His master's voice." The school had a number of records that provided some songs for our musical activities. Wooden needles were used to help from scratching the vinyl records. The entire student body would sing along with the songs on the records. I do not remember any of the songs we sang in that way. They must not have been memorable.

I do remember some recorded music that my sisters played during summer when we could borrow the record player from the school, and my sisters could bring records home from their 4-H meetings. These records gave me my first introduction to concert hall music—Edvard Grieg's "Peer Gynt Suite." The 4-H programs were designed, in part, to introduce Iowa farm girls to experiences that ran beyond the basics of rural Iowa farm life.

For what might have passed for dramatic arts, our country school would put on a program for the community at Christmas time every year. We created a stage and some backstage rooms by hanging black curtains on wire across the back of the school room. The program usually consisted of individually recited pieces, some group songs, and an occasional act of some kind. I do recall performing one act with a girl in the school. I came on stage for that act while puffing on a corncob pipe filled with talcum powder. My lines to sing were: "Rachel, Rachel, I've been thinking what a great world this would be, if the girls were all transported far beyond the northern sea." She would repeat the lines with "Reuben" and "boys" inserted instead of "Rachel" and "girls." After each line, we would hook arms and do a little circular dance to the same tune. Since I remember the little act so clearly, I assume that I enjoyed doing it, although I never thought of acting as a career.

My first grade teacher had special interest in singing and acting. She created a trio by putting together my three oldest siblings—my brother and two sisters. The trio must have been successful because they were scheduled to sing at a number of places around the county, including the Sac County Fair, which was a major event. My sister, Helen, tells of an experience the trio once had. After the trio sang a song, they were clapped back. Since the trio knew only one song—I think it was "Whispering Hope"—my brother and sister Helen sang a duet. They, too, were clapped back. But the duet knew only one song, so Helen sang a solo. As Helen recalls the story, she quips that she was not clapped back.

Early Signs of Ham

In my first grade, the teacher had me recite a declamatory piece for county contests. Evidently I was good enough to take part in the declamatory contest at the county level. I recall that we got to the program location late, and one student was already reciting her piece on stage. We noticed that there was an empty chair on the stage, so we reasoned that the chair was for me. I quietly went onto the stage and took the chair even while another student was speaking her piece. Rude!

As I sat on the chair—my feet dangling above the floor—I was trying to figure out how I would know when it was my turn. An older boy next to me finished his piece and sat down. I just sat there. Then the boy on the other side of me nudged me and told me it was my turn. When I tried to get off the chair, it fell over against me. I turned around, picked up the chair, and proceeded with my declamatory piece.

The piece was in the humorous category. I believe the title was "Old History Lesson." Basically it was an account of how a student tried to find ways to avoid doing the lesson—including chasing a fly. In spite of falling off the chair—or perhaps because of falling off the chair—I did get third place in that category. I recall getting a nice thermos bottle as a prize. My Dad found the thermos handy for hot coffee when he was doing field work.

My following teachers had less interest in music and declamatory work so my acting career was cut short. At any rate, I do not recall ever being interested in such a career. Life led me in other directions. One of my Dad's neighbors seemed to have a clearer vision of where the future might lead me. He once told my dad that I would either be a preacher or a professor. Bingo!

A Cute Country School Girl

I did not become romantically interested in women until I was in my late teens. This was probably because my hormones kicked in rather late. Nevertheless, in countryschool there was one girl that produced in me certain portents of things to come. She was two years younger than I and had pretty blue eyes. I do not recall any particular exchanges during school hours that reflected boy-girl feelings.

I do remember once, when I was about ten years old, a neighbor boy and I played with that girl in the haymow of our barn. They were on our farm because their fathers were helping my dad with grain harvest. It was the only time that we played in our barn.

There was never any physical contact of any kind, just a playful bit of romping around on the hay. I do remember, however, that I developed a certain heart-felt fondness for her during that episode. It was not an event that deserved description in a popular magazine, but it was memorable in its own way.

That feeling might have been mutual. Several decades later, after we were both married and were parents, I happened to meet her at the new swimming pool in Odebolt. She was inside the fence watching her children play. I was outside the fence just observing the new Odebolt facility. She came over to the fence when we discovered that we had this chance to meet after many years. I do not recall much of our conversation, but she did say, "I remember when we played in your barn." So she remembered also.

Not Great, but a Good Start

In retrospect, I would be inclined to suggest that my eight years in countryschool were not challenging in any meaningful way. I do not recall ever reading a book or writing a report on a book that I had read. It may be that my memory just fails me at that point. But those years were kind to me in many ways. At least I did not get disheartened by the educational venture. In the many years ahead, when I remained in school at a variety of levels, I always found the years more challenging but also enjoyable. There is so much to learn. Beginning with Clinton #3, Iowa country schooling—with its obvious limitations—was good to me and for me.

Three Brothers
Karl Emil, Johan Gustaf, Ernst Wilhelm Johannesson
Taken after Ernst's arrival in Iowa

The Iowa That Was

Odebolt, Iowa, Main Street, 1940. Cracker Jack granary in the distance.

1936 photo: Model T Ford truck and the Johnson children.
Left to right: Virginia, Howard, Helen, Elaine, Wayne.

Clinton No. 3 Country School, Sac County, Iowa, 1938. Back row: Kenneth Wingert, Virginia Johnson, Beverly Boerner, Elaine Johnson, Donald Wetzstein. Front row: Cletus Wingert, Charles Lange, Douglas Boerner, Wayne Johnson. Note: The Wingert boys are both barefoot.

5

The Little Church that Nurtured Me

"Jesus wants me for a sunbeam to shine for Him each day."
—SUNDAY SCHOOL SONG

IN MANY COMMUNITIES, individual churches tended to reflect national or ethnic roots. This was certainly true of the church that first nurtured me—the Evangelical Mission Covenant Church of Odebolt, Iowa. The membership list reflected its ethnic background: Anderson, Larson, Johnson, Linman, Lindskoog, Dahlquist, and Hokanson. The two pastors I remember were both Andersons. A Schmidt also got onto the membership roll—by marriage. The little church in town had its origins in the Mission Covenant Church of Sweden founded in 1878. That Church broke away from the Lutheran State Church of Sweden. It was part of a pietistic movement which found the State Lutheran Church to be too cold and formal. The Odebolt church was one of many churches established in the United States by Swedish immigrants. While the Mission Covenant Church was never large, it is known in the Chicago area for founding the Swedish Hospital and North Park College.

Our church building was a white wooden structure and a modest replication of the famous New England churches. It was a two-story building with only the sanctuary on the top floor and a kitchen and fellowship hall on the lower floor. There was no church office, but the pastor's residence was on the lot next to the church building. Sunday School classes for the younger children were held in the fellowship hall.

Theologically, the church would be classed as Fundamentalist in that it reflected a high inspiration view of the Bible. The Sunday School classes told the stories of Adam and Eve and the Flood as if they were actual historical events. Probably most members of the church believed that to be the case. Sermons reflected the same perspective. I do not recall that any of our pastors preached sermons that emphasized Heaven and the fear of Hell as Billy Graham did in his early crusades. The sermons in our Odebolt church were usually gentle and kind, with no looming threats.

Sin was taken seriously, with minor sins related to smoking, alcohol, and the movies. Movies were generally seen as the Devil's Church. Divorce was considered to be a moral failure of high degree, and children born out of wedlock were scandalous. I am not certain that the church believed that non-Christians went to Hell, though that would have been consistent with the basic theology. There was one Jewish husband and wife in Odebolt, and I do not recall that anyone asserted that they were destined for Hell. It may well be that many of our members were, at heart, closet Universalists.

As a child attending church, I probably did not pay much attention to the sermons. My mind would wander in various directions, and I recall that I used to count the tiles that covered the ceiling of the sanctuary. This pastime may have presaged my interest in math later in life. None of our pastors raised their voices during their sermons, nor did they gesticulate physically. The only specific statement that I remember from our pastors was his assertion that "Christians do not always have to have long faces like cows." It prompted some chuckles from the congregation.

A Singing Church

I have warm memories of the church as a singing church. Our choir was small but was made up of several families with truly gifted voices. Our Sunday School classes included little songs that expressed happiness, love, and loyalty. A typical song: "Jesus loves me this I know, for the Bible tells me so. Little ones to him belong. They are weak but he is strong."

At various religious seasons of the year, the children would come to the front of the sanctuary and sing for the congregation. The programs, of course, were warmly received by the adults, and the children felt loved and accepted. The reception to our singing may have also bolstered our egos a bit. While I never had formal music lessons, I have always enjoyed singing. At Iowa State College, I sang in a college octet and the college mixed chorus, as well as a number of barbershop quartets. The little church helped me to develop a love for vocal music.

It is difficult to evaluate just how devout I might have been as a child. I often said the goodnight prayer: "Now I lay me down to sleep, I pray thee Lord my soul to keep. If I should die before I wake, I pray thee Lord my soul to take." I do not recall having much of a fear of death, and I felt basically free of sin—as I understood it. At thirteen, I gave myself over to Christ, along with two other boys in the catechism class in the presence of our pastor. I recall that as a moving experience.

The First Baptist Church, Ames, Iowa

During my first year of college at Iowa State, I attended the First Baptist Church of Ames, Iowa. That church and its pastor would be considered to be "liberal." Ronald Wells, the pastor, held a PhD degree from Columbia University. It was at that church where I moved away from an infallible view of scripture. That move came easily since I had long held doubts about the historicity of the Flood and other events related in the Bible. The Ames church was an important part of my religious journey. A religious world view was still important to me, but I had moved away from the fundamentalism of the little church that first nurtured me. That little church had imbued in me a deep sense of the significance of religious faith. That sense is still with me although the content of my faith has shifted.

6

Labor Intensive Farming

WITH NO TRACTOR OR ELECTRICITY in the early 1930s, manual labor and long work days were the order of the day during growing season. In a curious way, however, we were essentially independent since we needed little help from other persons or businesses. We had our own water supply by way of well and windmill, our own fuel supply by way of wood and corncobs, and much of our food supply by way of chickens, dairy cattle, hogs and family garden. The house came with the rented farm. Farmers often worked with neighbors in joint efforts at some harvesting. Food not grown or butchered was purchased from grocery stores in Odebolt. Sugar, flour, coffee, and breakfast cereals were on the grocery list. Our family actually won a fine football because we bought the most Wheaties in a local grocery store contest. When others learned that the Johnson tribe was gunning for that football, they may have just thrown in the towel in the contest.

When Colorado peaches became available at the stores, we would buy them by the crate, and Mom would can them for future use. During winter season we would sometimes enjoy oyster soup made from purchased oysters, and at Christmas time we regularly had lutefisk—in honor of our Swedish roots. I must confess that the only way I could eat lutefisk was to bury it in mashed potatoes with lots of gravy.

Making Hay

Making hay was labor intensive. The first step was to cut the hay with a horse-drawn mower when the hay was ready for harvest. After the hay had dried, it was raked into rows by another horse-drawn mechanism. When sufficiently dry, the hay was loaded onto a hay wagon by means of a hay loader. Men rode in the hay wagon and arranged the hay being delivered into stacks that filled the wagon. The hay wagon and loader were both drawn by a team of horses. The hay was brought from the field to the barn in the hay wagon. The hay was then lifted into the upper level of the barn—the hay mow—by a strong rope that ran through a series of pulleys and was attached to some large forks on one end. These forks were driven into the hay on the hay wagon by the farmer. Once the hay forks were in place, a team of horses would pull on the other end of the rope, thus hoisting the hay into the barn. All in all, this was a clever series of mechanisms which saved an immense amount of basic labor. The hay bailer was another laborsaving device that came onto the scene in the 1940s. Laborsaving devices came onto the scene, but farming, as I knew it, was highly labor intensive.

Picking Corn

Hybrid corn was not extensively in use during my years on the farm. Dad would choose the best ears of corn from the fall crop, dry them out on a rack, and use the seed for the next year's plantings. Commercial fertilizers were not yet in vogue, so the field crops were nourished with manure gathered from the chickens, pigs, cows, and horses and spread over the fields. Nor were herbicides in use, so the weeds that grew in the cornfields were removed by cultivating between the corn rows at least twice each growing season. We counted it as a good year if the corn yielded 80 bushels per acre. With modern farming techniques—hybrid corn, genetic tinkering, commercial fertilizers, abundant rain, and herbicides—corn yields now average around 175 bushels per acre. Record yields of 600 bushels per acre have been recorded.

Picking corn by hand was something akin to a task and an art. Before mechanical corn pickers came on the scene, the corn was picked by hand, one ear at a time. In my early years there were corn-picking contests throughout Iowa. Rows of corn were lined up and the competing corn pickers would take their place at one end. Upon a signal, the contestants would work their way down the rows of corn until the contest time was over. The winner, of course, had the most corn in the wagon at the end of the contest. Along with horseshoes and the heaving of heavy iron weights—a manly art—corn picking was among Iowa farm athletics.

Dad, with the help of Mom some years and Howard, when he was big enough to help, picked corn by hand most years on that farm. When the corn in the field was sufficiently dry, Dad would hitch a team of horses to a large wagon with a box large enough to hold many bushels of corn. On the side of the wagon opposite to the pickers was a "bang board." Each ear of corn had to be wrested from the stalk on which it grew, and also stripped of all the husks around the ear. Only the bare ear was thrown into the wagon. In order to spare his hands, Dad would wear a pair of strong, soft gloves that were sometimes tarred in order to save wear on the gloves. He also wore a hook that was strapped to one of the gloves. This hook was used to tear the husks off of the ear of corn in an expeditious manner. As each ear was picked, it was thrown against the bang board and then fell down into the wagon box.

The horses completely understood the process. With a signal from Dad, they would pull the wagon ahead a few yards and then wait as he made his way up the row of corn. I was never large enough to be of much help in the process, although I often tagged along when both Mom and Dad were picking. When I got tired, I would crawl into the wagon box—near the front where I was least apt to be hit by ears of corn being hurled into the wagon. The entire process was, of course, labor intensive. When Dad's health faltered in the 1940s, he hired a neighbor to help harvest the corn with a tractor-mounted mechanical corn picker.

Harvesting Oats

Oats was one of our main cash crops but was mostly used to feed the horses and sometimes finely ground for use as food for hogs and chickens. This was also a labor intensive product. As warmer weather arrived in the spring, the land to be planted to oats was either plowed or disked and then "dragged" in order to provide a smooth surface for planting. As I recall, the oat seed was scattered over the field with a mechanical device and was then raked under with a horse drawn rake.

When the grain was ripe, it was harvested in a series of moves. First, the grain was cut and tied into bundles with the horse drawn "binder." The bundles were then placed, by hand, into small stacks, grain side up, so that the grain could dry. When dry, the bundles were then tossed with a pitch fork into a hay wagon. When full, the wagon was drawn by horses to a threshing machine place near the barn lot. This was a large machine driven by a wide belt powered by a large tractor. Farmers would pitch the bundles, one by one, into the conveyor on the threshing machine. The machine would strip out the grain and then blow the straw out of the other end. This harvesting was always done as a neighborhood event. A local farmer owned the threshing machine and other farmers would pay him for the use of the machine on their crop. Several neighboring farmer would help each other during this harvest. They would move from farm to farm with their own horses and wagons and help each farmer bring the grain in from the field. I remember the large noon meals that Mom would prepare for the farmers who helped Dad harvest our grain.

This rather extended process was shortened some years later when grain "combines" came into use. This machine cut the standing grain while it was standing, removed the oats and disposed of the straw all in one operation. This saved an enormous amount of labor. The machines were costly, so not every farmer owned one.

Dad did not. Those who managed to buy a combine would help neighboring farmers with their grain at some standard fee. Soy beans were harvested entirely with combines later in the fall when the beans were dry enough for harvest.

The Livestock

The births of newborn piglets and calves were major events and crucial for our farm economy. Watching baby chicks peck their way out of the eggshell in which they grew was also a wonder to behold. But birthing had its own risks. Sows delivered their piglets while the sow was lying down. Without any help from their mother, the newborn piglets would find their way to the mother's teats and begin to nourish themselves. Unfortunately, sometimes a sow in a pen with her new litter would lie down on one of her piglets. Usually the piglet could squeal and the mother would move, but sometimes the piglet was unable to sound the alarm and died under its mother's weight.

Malformed calves were sometimes born dead or died quickly. The birthing of these malformed calves was often difficult. On one occasion Dad rescued a calf after the mother gave birth to her normal offspring out in an open field on a cold and wintry day. Evidently Dad became aware of the missing cow and went to look for her. He found her in the field with the calf fully born. But the calf was lying on the snowy ground, evidently unable to get up. It was in danger of freezing in the cold. Dad picked up the calf in his arms and led the mother back to the barn. The calf probably weighed 60 to 70 pounds. Dad took the almost lifeless calf into our kitchen and laid it behind the kitchen stove to help warm it up. In the middle of the night, the calf began to recuperate and stirred behind the stove. Then Dad took the calf back to the barn and reunited it with its mother. The calf, now able to stand, began having its first meal of mother's milk.

In contrast to modern farming—which usually focuses on raising many head of one kind of livestock—our livestock consisted of a few beef cattle, some milk cows, a dozen or two pigs, and a cluster of chickens. The chickens provided us with eggs to eat and enough extra eggs to sell in town. The chicken flock also provided the critters for our chicken dinners. We sold our beef cattle and most of our hogs to beef and pork plants. Dad would butcher a hog at least once a year to provide for some meat in our diet. Since we did not have any means of refrigeration, Mom would can much of the pork in glass jars. Occasionally some ducks and sheep were added. Our dairy cows were milked by hand. The milker would sit next to the cow on a one-legged stool and draw milk by squeezing the teats on the cow's udder and directing the milk into a milk pail. Some cows seemed to resent the process and would occasionally kick the milk bucket or the farmer. A chain hobbler would be used on those cows to prevent their antics. All five of us children learned to milk, but seldom were all those hands needed. We had one gentle Jersey cow that patiently allowed all of us to learn on her equipment.

Milking the Cows

Milking cows by hand was a tedious and boring task. With my head pressed against the cow's side, I had time to think about the day's schedule and what recreation might come to pass. Our farm cats would usually be standing by in the barn waiting for a serving of fresh milk when we were finished. Sometimes a cat would get an advance taste when I squirted milk in the direction of the cat. The cat would attempt to catch some of the milk in its mouth as the stream passed by. That effort at some form of recreation was not altogether a waste of milk, but perhaps a waste of time.

From the milk cows, we got the milk we drank and the cream for coffee, cooking, and making butter and ice cream. Extra cream was sold to a dairy in town. A hand- driven "separator" was used to separate the cream from the milk. Our homemade ice cream was truly ice *cream*.

7

Horsepower on the Farm

Dad loved his horses. How could you not but love those huge but gentle creatures who worked for you from sunrise to sunset, in heat and cold, without complaint. I still find it difficult to understand just why these large animals submit themselves to the control of such little creatures as human beings.

Although I was too young to drive a team of horses, I recall their names. Cap was our riding horse as well as a work horse. Barney, light brown in color, was a huge animal, our largest horse. Then there were Maude and Kate. Kate was the smallest and tended to lag behind when she was on a working team. Later we acquired another horse, Prince, who truly deserved his name. A large, dark animal that was always ready to do the work asked of him.

Sleeping Sickness Hits: We Lose Big Barney

A personal as well as financial loss hit our farm in the late 1930s when a disease, Eastern equine encephalitis, commonly called Triple E or sleeping sickness, moved through Iowa. The disease seems to have been spread by a particular breed of mosquitoes.

Dad lost at least three of his horses, including Barney, Cap, and Maude. When a large farm animal died, such as a horse, we would call the rendering works. They would come to the farm with a big truck and with a pulley drag the dead animal onto the truck bed. The flesh of the animals was processed into something we called tankage, a high protein feed used for pigs.

My dad was especially attached to big Barney. When Barney fell ill, and it became certain that he would not survive, Dad and Mom decided to call the rendering works. Dad was not home on the farm when the rendering truck came to get Barney. My belief was that Dad could not stand to see his devoted horse shot and then dragged away. When the rendering-works truck and driver arrived, Mom showed him which horse was to be taken away. The driver led Barney out of the barn to an open area. Then he shot Barney in the head and hauled him onto the truck. It was, perhaps, an act of mercy since it ended Barney's suffering. But Dad chose not to witness the merciful deed.

Enter: The John Deere Tractor

The loss of the horses by disease brought our farm into the tractor era. Dad purchased a 1939 Model B John Deere tractor with rubber tires in front and steel lugs instead of rubber tires in back—the traction wheels. It was rated to have twelve horsepower on the drawbar. It may be that the rubber traction tires would have increased the cost of the tractor beyond my parents' reach. But the steel lugs served very well, and there were no hard surfaces, like concrete, that would make lugs inconvenient. The John Deere did not have a self-starting mechanism. To start the engine, the farmer had to spin a fly-wheel by hand until the engine fired.

The new tractor changed farm operations in a number of ways. For instance, the tractor made it possible to get more work done in a shorter time. With horses, we could cultivate only one row of corn at a time and at the pace the horses set. The new John Deere made it possible to cultivate two rows of corn at the same time and at a higher speed that the tractor could maintain.

The John Deere made loud popping noises as it ran and may have contributed to loss of hearing for myself and my older brother in later years. One fond memory is that of hearing my brother singing in his clear tenor over the sound of the tractor as he plowed the corn rows. This may have been an attempt to turn a boring job into something like an art form.

The shift from horses to tractor now made the farmer dependent on another aspect of the economy. With horses alone, a farmer could raise the oats and the hay needed to feed the horses. Of course, the acreage needed to raise the hay and grain to feed each horse costs the farmer since he cannot use those acres for cash crops. (I am using the masculine pronoun when referring to farmer, since that was the basic pattern in my childhood.) But with a tractor the farmer must buy the gasoline and the oil needed to run and maintain a tractor. He has lost some independence.

8

The Farmer's Wife: My Mom

"A man may work from sun to sun but a woman's work is never done." That old axiom clearly described my mother's life, although my father would often work after dark as well. In addition to her regular household labors, Mom sometimes helped to pick corn when it was harvested by hand. But a woman's work was for the women. I do not recall that Dad ever helped with house chores. But by the time I was old enough to remember, my three sisters were old enough to be of great help. And I do remember helping to wash dishes at the kitchen sink. As a married man and father, I never had any inhibitions about helping with household work and cooking. Time moves on.

Laundry Day

Laundry day was a prime example of the labor intensive nature of a family farm. With no running water in the house and no electricity, Mom washed the family clothes by heating water in a copper boiler placed on the kitchen stove. Small loads of laundry were done by hand on a scrub board placed in a wash tub. Laundry soap was homemade by using a recipe of lye and fat rendered from butchered pigs. Larger loads were washed in a washing machine located in a small building some twenty feet off the kitchen door. After heating the water on the kitchen stove, Mom would lug it to the washing machine.

The first washing machine that I remember was powered by a big gasoline engine that turned the washing machine with a belt. The engine was known as a "hit-and-miss" engine and was used on farms for a variety of tasks. The speed of the engine was controlled by a mechanism that cut off the gasoline supply when running too fast and opened the supply as the engine slowed; hence, the name "hit-and-miss" developed. The engine would "coast" when the gasoline supply was cut off. A large flywheel kept the engine going between the firings of the piston.

The tub of the washing machine itself was made of wooden slabs bound together by iron straps. The machine also had a ringer that helped to get water out of the clothes before they were hung up outside to dry. Clothes were air dried, even in winter. Mom got a newer model of washing machine in the late 1930s. It had the more modern steel and enamel tub. Since we did not yet have electricity, the wash machine was powered by a small Briggs and Stratton gasoline engine mounted on the machine. Later, when we got electric service, the gasoline engine was replaced by an electric engine. Going modern!!

Some of the newly washed and dried clothes also needed to be ironed. I believe the sheets—hung out to dry—did not need ironing since they were acceptably soft and smooth. But shirts, dresses, trousers, handkerchiefs, table linens, etc., did require ironing. Before electricity and an electric iron, Mom ironed clothes by using heavy irons made of iron—hence the term "ironing." The iron, itself, was heated by placing it on the heated kitchen stove. The hot iron was carried with a detachable wooden handle. Mom would work with one iron while a second was heating on the stove. Again, no thermostatic control, so care had to be taken not to burn the item being ironed. So ironing was an art as well as a labor.

We dressed simply. During the summer I lived basically in a pair of overalls without a shirt. This minimal covering resulted in cases of rather severe sunburn on some occasions. I doubt that I even wore underwear. Going barefoot served well except in the wintertime. With chickens ranging freely around our yard, however, going barefoot during summer was of some risk. There were times when my kind older sisters would help me clean my toes after an encounter with chicken droppings. I could not stand the smell. I do not recall wearing hand-me-downs, probably because my brother was eight years older and his clothes were not saved while three sisters were born. No doubt my younger sisters had hand-me-downs from older sister, Helen. While Mom patched many clothes and darned many a sock, I do not recall that she sewed any clothes that I wore, although she made some clothes for my sisters. Mom used a Singer sewing machine that was operated by a foot pedal. The machine was a clever invention and was useful for a variety of sewing tasks.

Baking: Farmer's Wife's Craft

The local grocery stores aided the farm wives by having an abundant supply of flour in 40-pound bags and sugar in even larger bags. Mom would bake a variety of breads, donuts, pies and cakes. All this was done with her kitchen stove which was heated with corncobs or small sticks of wood and some occasional chunks of coal. There was no thermostatic control of oven heat, but Mom managed to cook without burning or undercooking the food. When coming home from country school, we were often greeted by the great smell of freshly baked goodies.

The making of donuts was a special event. After rolling the dough into a flat sheet, the donuts were cut out and placed directly into a pan of boiling grease, probably from hog tallow. When fully raised, the donuts were rolled around on a plate of powdered sugar. It was difficult to wait until they were cool enough to eat.

My mother's cooking was truly labor intensive as all farming generally was in those days. As my brother, my three sisters, and

I grew, we took part in all the farming and food preparation. The chance to take part in all these work related activities gave a sense of belonging and significance to even a small child.

9

How We Ate

I have never eaten as well as I did at family gatherings when I was a boy. This may be a romanticized memory, but I do think it is true. Once or twice a year we would gather at one of my aunt's home for a royal feast of a great spread of home cooked food: ham, turkey, mashed potatoes and gravy, scalloped potatoes, vegetables, salads, and a variety of cookies, cakes, and pies. I always took more than I could eat—but ate it anyway. One of my aunts seemed to consider these feasts to be something like a cook-off contest with her sisters. Mom was not competitive by nature, nor jealous, but she held her own at those events. Eating was one of the joys of my childhood but fortunately not the only joy.

We never ate out as a family. Few families around Odebolt did in those days, and the little town had only one place that could have been considered to be something like a restaurant—the Modern Inn. It was also one of the few places in town where beer was served. However, given my nurturing in an abstaining tradition, I had no inclination to locate other sources. Some of my high school friends knew where to find them.

No doubt our limited income was a major reason for not eating out as a family. This income level was also reflected in the fact that we never took family vacations. The family gatherings at aunts and uncles took the place of vacations. Any lengthy stay away from the farm would have been difficult, at any rate, since chores needed to be done everyday and the cows milked twice a day. As far as I recall, I do not think that any of our farmer neighbors took vacations either. Life was good but modestly lived.

On Alcohol

Our alcohol use was modified in a variety of ways. During prohibition, Dad and Mom made beer on the farm. Dad also kept a bottle of whiskey in the back cupboard and would take a small "swig" from time to time. Once, when a cousin and I went with the men from a family gathering into town, the men each had a beer. I was probably around eight years of age. My cousin and I were each offered a small glass of the brew. We no doubt thought of it as a kind of an early initiation into the ranks of manhood. That early introduction to this beverage made me realize that one had to learn to like beer. I am still of the opinion that many drink beer, not because they like it, but because it is "what one does." Wisconsin culture doubles down on that theme.

Alcoholic beverages were never part of our family meals. We were largely inclined toward "meat and potatoes." This was made possible by the variety of chickens and ducks we raised, along with pigs that Dad butchered. Beef cattle were too large for us to butcher on our own. Having no refrigeration available, Mom would can much of the pork that we butchered. Even when we finally had electricity on the farm, we never had a refrigerator.

Basics: Meat and Potatoes

Chicken was the most common meat on the table. Usually one of my sisters or my brother would catch what we needed for a meal from the flock that wandered quite freely around our yard. Mom often had the task of lopping off the chicken's head with an axe.

Given her rather grim facial expression, it was clear that she did not relish the task. Our chicken flock also supplied us with enough eggs for our needs and some extra that dad could sell to a grocery in town.

Potatoes were abundant. We would plant a good-sized plot of spuds in the spring and harvest them when the tubers were mature enough to store in our cellar. Harvesting potatoes was an annual event. A team of horses would pull the potato plow which unearthed the spuds and shook them largely free of dirt. The potatoes kept nicely in our dark and cool cellar for almost a full year.

The Summer Garden

Summer meant more variety in our food. All of us took part in caring for our vegetable garden which yielded an abundance of tomatoes, radishes, carrots, peas, cucumbers, squash, cantaloupe, and onions. Near the end of summer, we would feast on sweet corn which was grown on a patch reserved for that variety. Our small dairy herd supplied us with the butter needed for the sweet corn dinners. We had fresh vegetables for much of the summer season, and Mom would can some extra tomatoes for later use.

In addition to our vegetable garden, Mom would plant flowers, and sisters Helen and Virginia had fine flower gardens of their own. Their garden plot was rectangular with a large circle in the middle. As I recall, tall castor bean plants were planted in the center of the circle to give a sense of dimension. The edges of the garden were lined with rocks that had been whitewashed. The gardens were, I believe, 4-H projects of my sisters and were always a joy to behold.

Some years we enjoyed planting and harvesting strawberries. One fine memory is that of making homemade ice cream to be served with the strawberries. We had rich cream from our dairy cows and would freeze the ice cream in our hand-cranked freezer stoked with small pieces of ice chipped from a larger chunk brought home from town on the bumper of our car.

Fruit Trees

Our farm had a rather large grove of mulberry trees which yielded nicely every fall. Some were large and white in color and were always the sweetest. Most were of a dark purple, and equally tasty. The trees were rather tall, and picking the berries one by one was tedious. Our usual approach to harvesting mulberries was to have four of us hold a sheet below the limbs holding the fruit. Then another one of us would shake the limb. When the fruit was fully ripe, the berries would come raining down onto the sheet. This approach also meant that we would have to separate various sticks and little creatures that fell down with the fruit. But Mom's mulberry pies made it all most worthwhile.

We tried planting some cherry trees at one time, but we ended up feeding flocks of robins which would get to the fruit before we managed to harvest very many. Rather than fight the robins, we resigned ourselves to the understanding that birds, too, must eat to live.

Wild strawberries and asparagus often grew along our rural roadways. They were evidently planted with the help of birds which had run the seeds through their digestive system. When picked at the right time, the asparagus was thick and juicy. If overlooked, the stalks grew long, thin, and tough. The wild strawberries were small, but of great flavor. We often ate them on the spot but took some home when the crop was abundant. At one time, my brother came down with a bad case of giant hives which was probably an allergic reaction to the wild strawberries we had enjoyed.

The Family Meal

We had our family meals around a table in the kitchen area. The table was just large enough to seat all seven of us. If memory serves me correctly, I think I stood at the table when I was a small child but tall enough to reach my plate. I did not mind standing since standing while eating was supposed to help me grow. Being the youngest and the smallest, I no doubt had a deep urge to catch up to the size of my siblings. By the time I had finished high school, I finally caught up with my brother Howard in height, and surpassed my sisters. A legend of some kind suggests that Swedes stay green a long time. This was true in my case. I was about five feet ten inches tall when I graduated from high school in l948. It took me several more years to reach my mature height of six feet two inches.

In summary: We always had plenty of good food. Add to this the company and support of a loving family, and I count myself as blessed.

10

Trapping, Hunting, and Fishing

"From the dust of the earth, from the common elementary fund, the Creator has made Homo sapiens. From the same material he has made every other creature, however noxious and insignificant to us. They are earth-born companions and our fellow mortals."

—JOHN MUIR

When I think of the suffering of those little creatures when we trapped them, I confess to some remorse. I don't think I could do it at my present age. But those were different times, and trapping is what young rural boys did at that time. More importantly, it was a source of income—meager as it was.

Bounty for Pocket Gophers

Pocket gophers were one of the main targets of our trapping. These creatures—about the size of a rat, but much cuter—would burrow holes that meandered underground. While burrowing their holes, they would stuff the dirt into the pockets they had on each side of their cheeks. When the pockets were full, they would come to the surface and empty the pockets. The mounds they created in this way were circular and gently sloping. The mounds were also clues as to where we would find a place to set a trap.

We did not trap them for their fur. Because the State of Iowa had considered gophers to be a problem for farmers and a danger to horses if they stepped in a gopher hole, Iowa offered a bounty for every gopher caught. Some years we would get five cents for each pair of feet. For a "good" year we would get ten cents a pair.

After catching and killing a gopher, we would cut off their front paws—their digging paws—and put them in a Prince Albert tobacco can with a good deal of salt added. We collected the bounty at a Sac County office. With no particular enthusiasm, the clerk at that office would dump the collection of feet on a piece of paper and count them out with a wooden stick. I did not know the term "body language" at that time, but I was aware that the clerk did not particularly enjoy that task. On a good day, I might have collected up to two dollars from the clerk.

The most successful means of catching a gopher was digging with a small spade until the "crossing" in the gopher's hole was found. It was usually close to the mound the gopher had made. The trap was then placed in the crossing with some attempt to camouflage the trap by sprinkling dirt on it. The opening was then covered by any earthy material that was available. Often, while trapping in the cow pasture, we could find dried up "cow plops" that would do nicely as a cover. The traps we used were single spring with a jaw spread of about four inches. The trap was designed for larger creatures but worked well for gophers if carefully used. No such trap is currently listed in Amazon. The trap closest to the one we used is the Duke #3 double-spring trap, used for larger animals.

Gophers had their own means of defense. Often, if the gopher had sensed some danger, it would "plug" the tunnel with dirt where the trap was set and completely bury the trap. Sometimes, when the gopher had one paw caught in the trap, the poor creature would gnaw off that paw and go free. At those times I both admired the little creature's courageous quest for life and also felt sympathy for this small earthy creature brother or sister of mine.

The most distressing memories I have of trapping gophers was that of the task of killing the little creature after having trapped one. I had to pull the trap out of the hole, dragging the gopher along. They have large front teeth that they would display in a menacing way. I was amazed at the amount of fight they displayed. We did try to put them "out of their misery" as quickly as possible with a club of some kind. Result: another pair of paws for our Prince Albert Tobacco can and either five or ten cents bounty.

Gophers in Iowa may now have less to fear because of a County Auditor in Charles City in 2013. After a trapper dumped a load of gopher feet on the Auditor's desk, she began to wonder whether or not this bounty made any sense at this date. There were few horses now used in farming that might be hurt by stepping into a gopher hole. The county was paying fifty cents a pair at that time. After a survey, she found that only nine of Iowa's 99 counties offered bounties on gophers. Evidently she brought the matter before the County Council for consideration. I believe they decided to drop the bounty.

Bad News: A Civet Cat

We would occasionally trap a creature which we had not intended to catch. One morning before school, sister Virginia and I were checking our gopher traps and discovered that we had civet cat in one of our traps. A civet cat is basically a small spotted skunk. The one we caught fought us off with its most effective weapon—that of a spray of disgusting aroma. My sister and I were wondering what to do when a neighbor friend of ours, on his way to school, stopped by to help out. With the help of a small fence post he found nearby, he managed to subdue the creature. We had no use for the dead creature since there was no market for civet cat pelts

Reeking with civet cat odor, my sister and I went home, washed up, and changed clothes before we went to school. My neighbor friend went directly to school, civet cat stench and all.

The teacher did not send him home but did seat him in the back of the school room and opened all of the windows. From time to time, she would go to the window for a breath of fresh air. When I looked back at my neighbor friend, he would greet me with a big grin.

The Badger

One other time we caught a creature we did not intend to catch: It was a badger. The badger is quite rare in Iowa. It is related to the weasel family but much larger than weasels. Some can reach 36 inches in length including the tail. One morning, while checking our traps, my sister and I noticed that the area around one trap we had set was torn up by some creature. When we got close to the trap we noticed that the trap chain was very taut and that the creature in the trap was deep in the hole. We decided this was a job for Dad. We went home to tell him about our catch. He came out with us armed with a small baseball bat. He had guns but preferred to use a weapon that would not damage the pelt.

When dad arrived at the scene, he knelt down near the hole and gave the chain a tug. At that point the badger came roaring out of the hole, teeth bared and ready to fight. Dad managed—with some luck—to stun the badger with the baseball bat. If Dad had missed, he could have been badly mauled by the creature. The episode resulted in a lovely badger pelt added to our collection of furs.

The Skunk

We also trapped skunks that provided some income since a skunk pelt was worth about three dollars—a substantial amount in those days. After trapping these creatures, we would skin them and stretch their pelt over a shaped board or heavy wire. When the pelt was dry, we could sell the pelt to a local dealer. The skunk odor was gone by the time we sold the pelt.

My brother Howard trapped skunks before I was old enough to try. When he entered high school, I began to trap them. Skunks are surprisingly docile creatures. There are stories about a Game Warden who came upon a trapped skunk when it was not trapping season. The Warden gently released the skunk from the trap. The skunk licked its sore paw and then limped away without raising any stench at all. The skunks we trapped would retreat into the hole where they had been trapped, but they would often not use their odor weapon even when they were gently tugged out of the hole. My brother would then kill them with a shot through the head with his 22 rifle so not to damage the valuable fur. Then the skunk would release its stench weapon.

Skunk odor has a way of clinging. My brother, after he had skinned a skunk, cleaned up, changed clothes, and went with our father to a nearby town. While there, he was browsing in a rather nice clothing store. He happened to be near some women who were also shopping. One of the women said to the other, "Do I smell skunk?" At that point, my brother retreated quietly to another part of the store.

Muskrats and Mink

While I never trapped muskrats, my brother trapped them in a river some two miles away. Muskrat fur is elegant—thick and warm with a lovely brown color. They were the best source of money we could get from trapping. Muskrats were caught by placing a trap under water at the end of slides that the muskrats would make from the river bank into the river.

A mink pelt could be worth some sixteen dollars at the time, but minks were rare in our area. Over the years, we did catch two of the lovely creatures. Mink are in the weasel family and are a danger to poultry since they are voracious and natural killers. It was probably a mink that killed all of my mother's chicks she was raising on our back porch. This was after my father had died, and we had moved into a little house in Odebolt. I think my mother was raising the chicks to keep in touch with her farming background.

One morning, she discovered that all of the chicks she was raising had been killed by some creature. Creatures in the weasel family will often kill many more chicks or ducks than they need for food. They seem to go on a killing frenzy. Some time later I caught a mink in a stream not far from where we lived. It might well have been the creature that killed my mother's chicks.

The fur of a mink that we caught was thick and deep brown in color. Mink now raised on a mink farm may have white to black fur. They are used to make magnificent fur coats. Mink coats for women now sell from two thousand to four thousand dollars. They are clearly status coats. At this point in my life I am glad that there is strong social resistance to the sale of any coat made by the skin of animals.

Hunting Rabbits and Pheasants

Hunting was also a common activity on an Iowa farm. My father's hunting weapon was a twin-barrel 12-gauge shotgun. He also had a 32-caliber five-shot revolver that was not much larger than my father's hand. I do not recall when I first shot the 12-gauge shotgun, but I must have been ten years or more because it gave recoil that would substantially jolt the shoulder. I also believe that the blast from that gun did result in impaired hearing in my older years.

My brother bought some other guns so that he could hunt with Dad. He bought a 16-gauge bolt-action shotgun, a 22-caliber bolt-action rifle, and 22-caliber revolver with a 9-inch barrel. The shotgun and rifle were used as hunting weapons, but the revolver had little practical use.

Pheasant hunting was the most productive in terms of food. There was usually a time of the year when hunting was allowed, and usually only the males could be taken. They were beautiful birds. Cotton tail rabbits were often taken as well. Rabbit meat was mild and quite tasty. There were no deer to hunt in Iowa at that time. As usual, we humans tended to be the top of the food cycle. We owe so much to our animal sisters and brothers.

Fishing: Learning Patience

As an adult, I had some reputation for being patient. That patience may have been related to my Scandinavian genes. On the other hand, it could also have been nurtured by the experience of farming. Nature has her own timing and cannot be hurried along. Perhaps the main training for my patience was the experience of fishing. The Boyer river flowed a few miles from our farm home, and a lake of some size was ten miles away. River fishing was largely limited to bullheads, a type of catfish, and an occasional carp. With some care, we could also land a crayfish. The crayfish, or crawdad, could not be hooked, but if would sometimes hang onto the bait with its pincers and could be gently lifted from the stream to the river bank. Lake View, on the other hand, also yielded some bluegill sunfish, crappies, and an occasional large mouth bass. But at both locations, fishing required a good deal of patience most of the time. We seldom brought home much of a catch, but all species were tasty when cleaned and fried. Bullheads were as tasty as the other game fish and were easier to eat since they had fewer small bones to worry about.

11

Sex Education on the Farm

The haymow in the barn as a laboratory?

On an Iowa farm, sexual activity is almost everywhere. For farm boys at the time, this activity was often observed but seldom talked about in the family. I do not recall ever talking about sex with my parents or with my siblings. There was some speculation that went on with neighborhood boys as we attempted to get a clear understanding of various terms—standard or slang—related to sexual activity. On an Iowa farm, however, sexual activity was almost always available to watch. Did that make Iowa farm boys—and girls—voyeurs of some kind? It would have been difficult to avoid observing sexual acts between farm animals. Hens and roosters provided the most common examples since they ran loose around the chicken house and nearby yards. It seemed difficult to transfer the sexual activity of chickens to human activity. The copulations of pigs and cattle were less available to observe and was limited to the fertility cycles of the sows and the cows. But their activity appeared to be more closely related to our human ventures.

Sex Education on the Farm

The Roosters Wasted No Time

The mating of hens and roosters was a curiosity of sorts but always seemed to be quickly accomplished with little or no mating rituals before the mating itself. The most striking example of this quick mating that I recall was when I found the dried up body of a hen in the upper floor of our barn. She had evidently been trapped in that area when the barn was loaded with hay. I took her dried and feathered corpse and flung it out of a top door of the barn. As soon as the corpse hit the ground, a rooster rushed over and mounted her. The act didn't last long. He soon dismounted and circled the corpse in some evident confusion.

The Larger Farm Mammals

The sexual activity of cattle and pigs was more robust. We had horses, but the males were rendered incapable of and disinterested in sexual activity. The females evidently went through fertility cycles, but we never brought over an active male for breeding purposes. As I recall, there were times when someone led this active male—a stud horse—down the road to a neighbor's farm where breeding was accomplished. I never observed the mating of horses on the farm, although many of us, as adults, have witnessed the activity on nature TV programs about wild horses.

While there seemed to be nothing like foreplay in the chicken flock, there was an activity that might deserve that name in the cattle yard. The bull would romance the cow until she seemed willing to be mounted. She did seem to be in control of the action. Females in nature often do. I am not certain that much "courting" goes on between a boar and a sow. The only such action that I do recall was when our boar relentlessly chased a sow around and around the pen area until she finally stopped, and he mounted her. All that foreplay must have excited the boar, since he suffered from a bad case of premature ejaculation and lost a good deal of semen before he managed penetration. Whether the sow stopped out of sheer fatigue or desire may have been a debatable point.

Piglets Get Castrated

None of the piglets born male on our farm arrived at adulthood in fully male condition. Boars were brought in from other lots to ensure crossbreeding. When our piglets reached a certain size, my father, with the help of my brother, would catch each of the little males and remove his testicles—castrating him. That was done with a few quick strokes of my father's well sharpened pocket knife and a dose of antiseptic—probably alcohol—to guard against infection. While the piglets resented being held down, they seemed not to endure much pain in the process. I doubt if they worried much about their future lack of sexual activity. As far as we were concerned, their future lay in loins and pork chops, not fatherhood. Our dog, Corky, was something like a special guest at castrating time. As the testicles were removed and tossed away, Corky would gobble them up. His appetite seemed to wane as the number of piglets castrated grew.

The Black Angus Bull

With our cattle herd, we kept a bull purchased from some breeder who had a reputation for good stock. Dad always preferred black Angus rather than Shorthorns, which were usually multicolored in white and red. While we had dairy cows, we never owned a dairy bull, such as Holstein or Jersey; this because Dad intended to raise beef cattle rather than dairy. Angus was our preferred beef type.

Our Angus bulls had a reputation of reasonably good nature in dealing with their human owners. While I was always cautious around the beasts, I do not recall that any in our family was ever threatened by one. Dairy bulls such as Holstein and Jersey, on the other hand, had a reputation of being dangerous.

While our Angus bull behaved well around his owner and family, he would occasionally engage in a fight with our neighbor's Shorthorn bull when a cow in our herd was ready for mating. One time the neighbor's bull broke through the barbed-wire fence and engaged in battle with our Angus for mating rights. As I recall, my dad ended the battle by going to the scene with a three-tine pitchfork and used it effectively on the rump of the neighbor's invading bull. The bull chose to leap back through the fence and head for safety. I still marvel at my father's courage since, pound for pound, he would have been no match for an angry Shorthorn.

Sex Education for Moderns

A generation later, an Iowa farm girl—now a trained nurse—used a more modern approach to sexual education for her children. She told one story about her teaching style. She had two boys, and then a girl. When the girl seemed old enough to be instructed in matters sexual, the mother decided to use straightforward description of just how children come to develop in the mother's womb. After telling her daughter about how the father's sperm gets into the uterus, the little girl was quiet for a while, thinking about herself and her two older brothers. Then she exclaimed, "You mean that you had to do that three times!!" Eventually, it seems that hormones overtake aesthetics. As philosopher David Hume once said, "Reason is and only can be the slave of the passions."

12

Our Values

WHILE OUR SWEDISH BACKGROUND was not conspicuously or overtly celebrated, it certainly was an important part of our identity. Swedish communities already in the United States helped make it possible for Swedes like my father and his brothers to immigrate. Local Swedish-rooted churches in the U.S., mostly Lutheran, linked with the Church of Sweden to assist in the immigration processes.

The Swedish language was also significant. While both of my parents spoke Swedish, we were never taught the language as children. No doubt this was understood as a legitimate aspect of becoming an American citizen. During WWI, foreign languages were sometimes looked upon as unpatriotic if not subversive. In retrospect, I now wish that I would have learned Swedish from my parents. Too many U.S. citizens are mono-linguistic. Pastors in our little local church were clearly Swedish in descent, but the sermons were always in English when I was part of the congregation. Some of the older preachers, when visiting, found that they needed to resort to their native tongue in order to express themselves adequately. When relatives from Sweden visited in our homes and communities, the visits were always marked by vigorous conversations in the native tongue. I vividly recall the "lilting" nature of the language on those occasions.

Ethnic Distinctions

Ethnic distinctions in the Odebolt area were largely expressed through the local churches. It was not so much that some persons were German, or Scandinavian, or Irish; instead, it was a matter of religious identity. Our Protestant connections prompted us to guard against things Roman Catholic. There seemed to be no outright hostility—just caution. Our preachers never railed against Romanism. It was clear, though not directly spoken, that we should guard against marrying one. This was a disadvantage in some ways since some of the Irish girls in town were quite attractive. No doubt the caution ran in both directions. Some of my country school classmates were Catholic, and when my friend visited our church service, he made certain that he did not participate in the service. He was clearly an observer.

Race was hardly a direct issue since Afro-Americans and Latinos were totally absent from our community. I do not recall any direct racial slurs or demeaning jokes. Nevertheless, racial overtones, stereotypes, and slurs were part of our rural culture. This was true even though many of us cheered Joe Louis on in prize-fight bouts. I do not recall that we ever wished for a "white" champion. Minstrel songs were often heard on radio broadcasts, and Al Jolson was popular. While a few Blacks were successful in minstrel music, those who most profited from the genre were white men done up in blackface.

More direct racial overtones were expressed in the use of the N word for a number of objects—as in N-head rocks and N-toe nuts. I have a rather vivid memory of a performance given by a girl in my country school at one school program for our rural community. She was made out in blackface and had just her face and arms protruding through a curtain. I recall only some of the opening lines: "I's my mommy's little saphire, Liz. I's about the cutest little nigger there is. With my bright green dress and my hair all curled, I's a pretty cute kid, I'll tell the world." That is one of only two acts that I recall from all the programs we put on at our country school over the eight years I attended; the other act was one where I was "Reuben" in a "Reuben and Rachel" skit. The lines about Liz have stuck with me, I believe, because I sensed something totally inappropriate in that little act. Our parental audience may have smiled, but I do not recall that anyone laughed. Nor do I understand the point of that particular piece in our school program. No doubt the act was a part of the racist overtones in rural Iowa at the time. I ran directly into racist cultural patterns when a black friend of mine at Iowa State College was humiliated when trying to rent an apartment for himself and his bride. A widow lady from First Baptist Church finally invited them into her home.

Discipline

It has been said that when children misbehave, German parents would say "Straighten up," French parents would say "Be wise," and Swedish parents would say "Be kind." My parents reflected the Swedish response. I do not recall any time when either my mother or father spanked any of us. A stern look or short lecture sufficed.

While I must have needed correction from time to time, I recall only once when I was directly reprimanded. Two of my sisters and I were smoking corn-silk cigarettes—dry corn-silk wrapped in a piece of newspaper—while hiding in our corncrib. We were playing some roles from a radio mystery series. Since the floor of the crib was concrete, it seemed reasonably safe. The problem with this procedure was that the paper would often flame out. My father saw some smoke curling out of the corncrib door and came to investigate. Smoking was not part of our family practice, and Dad gave us a stern lecture. He insinuated that smoking could lead to a downward moral spiral—and be a danger to farm buildings. That episode cured us of corn-silk cigarettes.

No member of the family ever took up smoking. At one time, however, a cigarette company sought to entice us into the habit by sending a small package of cigarettes in the mail. I was a bit surprised—and amused—by what occurred when that package arrived. My mother and at least two of my sisters lit up! Then they all posed as sophisticated women enjoying a smoke. None of them got hooked. My brother Howard escaped getting hooked while in the army even though cigarette companies "generously" supplied sample packets of cigarettes.

Our Swedish parents did not vocally urge us to be kind; they modeled kindness. Since there were no French in the area, I cannot comment on their possible use of "Be wise." We did have several German families in the area, and at least one incident illustrated the "Straighten up" attitude. I was working for a neighbor by driving his tractor during some harvesting. As his family and I were ready to leave for Odebolt one evening, his little toddler son came trotting in from the machine shed with a big smile on his face. He was probably some three years of age. The little lad and his clothes were badly messed up with black grease. His father gave him a spanking while the little boy cried out "Grease gun." I recall wincing as I looked on. The little boy was probably a bright and lively child making his way into the world. He also made another error in judgment when he caught a number of chickens and put them inside the family car. The hens had been there quite a while before the boy's mother discovered them. Having chickens loose in your auto for a number of hours is, of course, at some risk to the upholstery. We drove into town that evening with bath towels covering the auto seats. I do not recall that he was disciplined for that activity. He was a charming little boy finding ways to have fun on the farm.

Drinking and Smoking

Alcoholic beverages and smoking were generally frowned upon by our little church. I do not, however, recall that this concern was mentioned from the pulpit. While we avoided smoking, my parents were less concerned about alcoholic beverages. During the years of prohibition, my parents made beer. Dad also kept a bottle of whiskey in one of our pantry cupboards and he would occasionally take a "swig." The bottle lasted a long time. This teetotaling background stayed with me for years. In graduate school I came into a circle of drinking Lutherans and got converted.

Movies and Card Games

The local movie theatre was sometimes deemed as the "devil's church" by our congregation. Nevertheless, we attended that church on rare occasions. Our entire family attended once when a Swedish film in the Swedish language was shown. My parents and other Swedish speakers enjoyed the show.

Playing cards was associated with gambling. Nevertheless, we did have playing cards. One card game, Rook, was played with cards without the usual features. The game was sometimes referred to as "Christian cards." We also had a deck of regular cards and played solitaire, hearts, and five hundred—a game akin to bridge. These games provided family entertainment on cold winter nights. No gambling habits developed.

Swearing

Swearing was generally frowned upon. When I was about six years old an incident related to trapping gophers almost got me into trouble with the teacher. My older sister and I were trapping gophers on the school grounds. Instead of being of help, I was rolling on my stomach on a bent-up twenty-gallon barrel. I must have been meditating on some troubling matter, because all of a sudden I shouted out "s - - t." My sister looked shocked since I seldom if ever swore. Our teacher called to me from a school window. I trotted down to the schoolhouse steps not knowing what to expect. This teacher was always gentle and kind, but I had never cursed on the school grounds before. When the teacher confronted me, she looked at me sternly and then asked me if my father swore. I nodded that he did. The teacher just looked at me for a few moments and then went back into the school house. I should add that my father seldom swore, but he did at times when trying to corral a pig that had gotten out of its quarters. He never used the word that I used when he swore. Why I uttered it that day is still a mystery to me.

Sex

Sex, of course, was a major moral concern although seldom if ever directly discussed. I am not aware of what my mother may have told my sisters, but I never received any kind of education or advice. Farm animals, of course, provided something like uninhibited expression of the drive. I recall trying to widen my knowledge about sexuality by checking terms in the dictionary. The major problem in that research was that it tended to get circular. One word would refer you to another and that word would refer back again to the first.

Human beings have no doubt wrestled with the sex drive for thousands of years. While it is monumentally enticing, it seems to carry a dark side with it. Perhaps the power of the drive is, itself, unsettling. In his *Denial of Death*, Ernest Becker notes that sex is of the body, and the body is of death. Death is a major human problem. Plato, sometimes known as the father of Western philosophy, once observed that the body (soma) is the prison house (sema) of the soul. Human sexual expressions range all the way from total abstinence to orgies.

In our family, sex was openly affirmed in marriage, but there were overtones of danger and darkness about the topic. "The Fall" story of Adam and Eve in the Garden of Eden seemed to have had overtones of sex and linked sexuality to Original Sin. Our church taught that sex outside of marriage was deeply sinful, and pregnancy outside of marriage was an abomination. The latter was a rare occurrence in our community.

13

My Dad Dies

"Now I work never to forget how close to dying we are, how rare a gift is a life responsibly and fully, consciously lived, how the face and touch and embrace of someone you love and who loves you back is perhaps the furthest you can get from what death means."

—STEPHANI COOK

THROUGH ALL THE STAGES of my father's disease and decline, I do not recall that I ever thought that he might be dying. It may well be that we are unable to see that which is fearful. Dr. Elisabeth Kubler-Ross would call it "denial." For years my father had stomach problems and would take anti-acids like Alka-Seltzer to relieve the discomfort. In the fall of 1943 his health began to fail more dramatically. One day he had an intense attack of pain while I was home from school for lunch. It frightened me to see my dad in such misery. I tried to avoid the situation by going back to school, but my mother kept me at home suggesting that I might have to drive my father to the doctor's office. But a local doctor answered my mother's call and drove to our place. My father's pain settled

My Dad Dies

down somewhat just as the doctor arrived. I went back to school with a frightened and heavy heart. The local doctor seemed to have no idea of how to help my father. Medical care was extremely limited in those days.

All that fall, my father was not able to do the active things he had always done, such as picking corn. He hired a neighbor who had a corn picker mounted on his tractor to pick our corn. Neighbors were always ready to help a neighbor when the need arose. My brother had been drafted into the army in 1942 and was training in Kentucky. My older sisters and I gradually took over other chores such as feeding the livestock and milking the cows.

As my father's health began to fail, he was unable to do any farm work. Finally, he was confined to bed in a downstairs bedroom. I do remember that he had lost a good deal of weight and that his room seemed to reek of disease. Still, I never thought that my father might be dying. I am quite certain that my mother feared that, and that she shared it with my sisters if not my brother. My mother would have remembered that my father's younger brother died of cancer in his late twenties some decades earlier. The memory must have been painful for both my father and my mother during my father's developing illness.

A New Doctor Advises

In some hope of finding help, my mother finally called a physician from another town. Apparently he was quite direct with my parents and told them that my father should be transferred to the University of Iowa Hospital at Iowa City, Iowa, about 120 miles from home. My mother contacted an ambulance from our home town, but on the day it arrived, a major snow storm hit the area. The ambulance drivers indicated that it would be difficult to take my father in that weather, but my mother insisted. We dressed my father for the trip. My sister recalls how thin my father's feet were when she slipped on his shoes. The drivers helped him walk through the snow storm to the ambulance.

As it turned out, the drivers took my father to a hospital in Carroll, Iowa, which was much closer than Iowa City—only thirty miles away from our home. My father's stay at the Carroll hospital was just over a week, but he received good care and he mentioned how much he enjoyed the fish served on Friday. The plans to take him to Iowa City were still in place. In retrospect, I believe he was being sent to the University of Iowa Hospital, not because they could save his life, but because they would care for him there without cost. Iowa has a tradition of having safety nets for citizens in need. I would benefit by such a safety net some during my college years when I received care at the state tuberculosis sanatorium near Iowa City.

My Last Goodbye

I saw my father alive for the last time at that Carroll hospital. My father's brother Karl, my mother and my three sisters visited him on that day. Brother Howard was in the army. We knew that Dad would be moved to Iowa City soon. After a visit, we prepared to leave his room so that he could be alone with Mother. As I prepared to say goodbye to him, Dad held back tears and offered his hand. So I shook his hand. I do not recall that I said a word. Given our Scandinavian roots, we were not inclined to show affection in many ways—though we knew we were loved. I left his room along with Uncle Karl and my sisters. Uncle Karl wiped tears from his eyes. After some time my mother left my father's room, and we returned to our farm home. Even at that point, I could not bring myself to consciously acknowledge that my father might be dying.

The Telephone Call

My mother traveled by bus once to visit my father in the Iowa University Hospital. The painful news came by telephone several days after her return home. Dad had died. Evidently he was taken by a heart attack. A doctor talked to mother through her grief and

My Dad Dies

asked permission to do an autopsy. Mother refused. She could not bear the thought of having her husband's body cut up in some way. My sister drove mother and me to Odebolt to see our pastor. He was of great help in making various arrangements. A local funeral home was to bring my father's body back from Iowa City. The pastor helped mother send a telegram to my brother, who was in Kentucky serving in the army. The military failed my brother. Instead of finding a chaplain to bring the news to my brother, the telegram was just dropped on his bunk. It may be that the army did not know the message in the telegram. Howard read it when he came back from exercises. The news surely came as a shock to him since he had not expected Dad to die. I believe our Pastor went to our local high school to inform my sister, Elaine, who was still in school there.

My oldest sister was teaching a country school not far from our home. On the way to Odebolt to see our Pastor, we drove by her schoolhouse. She happened to be on the schoolhouse steps as we drove by. Later, she indicated that she knew why we were making that trip to town. Evidently she was more aware of Dad's impending death than I was.

Dad Laid To Rest

Following local tradition, my father's embalmed and casketed body was brought to our farm home. The casket was opened and placed in our living room. Just above the casket was an open hole in the ceiling designed for a stove pipe. My sisters and I could look down through the hole and see our dad lying in the casket. He looked peaceful and seemed to have a slight smile on his face. We found it consoling to see our dad finally at rest and no longer suffering from his disease and decline.

Neighbor men stayed with the body overnight and passed the night by playing cards. The men decided they should quit smoking their cigars because they heard someone coughing in an upstairs bedroom. The next day we had a short service at home. His body was then brought to our church where the funeral service was held. Typical of our Swedish cultural tradition, there was little grief openly expressed at the funeral. The Ladies Aid of the church served sandwiches, cake, and coffee in the lower level of the church after the funeral.

A Neighbor Widow Comforts Mom

There were two times when mother expressed her grief openly. The first was when she received the phone call from the University of Iowa Hospital informing her of Dad's death. The other time she openly expressed her grief was the night when our neighbors came to our house for something like a moving away party. We were soon to move into the town of Odebolt after our farm sale. As neighbors arrived, my mother greeted them with emotional reserve. Then one woman I did not recognize came in the door. When mother saw her, she quickly moved toward the woman and flung her arms around her, weeping. The woman held her close. Mother stayed near that woman all evening, drawing strength from her. The woman clearly reflected that strength. Later I learned that the woman's husband had died a year earlier. Mother knew that this was one person who truly knew her pain.

Neither I nor my four siblings expressed any open grief at the time of my father's death or at his funeral. Some of this, no doubt, was Scandinavian reserve. But it may also be that all of us knew that Dad was dying, and we went through something like preparatory grief. We grieved him while he was declining at home and while he was hospitalized. Dad had just turned fifty-six.

Life Without Dad

My life was changed enormously by my father's death. Since my brother was in the army, I became man of the house at thirteen years of age. I do think I took that role quite seriously. My farm life also ended after we moved into the town of Odebolt. I do not recall that I missed farm life at all. Perhaps what helped is that our little

My Dad Dies

dog, Corky, came into town with us bringing with him a touch of the farm life we once knew.

My father's death altered my life in another way. When my brother was discharged from the army after WWII, he went to college with the help of the GI Bill. With that help, he was able to get through to his Master's Degree in Agricultural Engineering at Iowa State University. He would no longer be in position to help on the farm. If my father had not died, he would have needed help on the farm when I graduated from high school. I would have faced a difficult choice: help Dad on the farm or go to college. Since I had no funding for college, I might have stayed on the farm. Since my father died, my farm roots were severed, and I was free to make life choices. I ended up spending a number of years in college as I moved through my Bachelor's Degree in Civil Engineering, my Bachelor's Degree in Ministry, and a Doctor of Philosophy from the University of Iowa. Life brings to us changes over which we have little or no control.

14

IN RETROSPECT

SOME EIGHTY-PLUS YEARS FROM my days as a farm boy, I now find myself amazed at the enormous changes that have taken place in Iowa farming. My country schoolhouse has long been gone—now probably being used as a grain storage building. All of the buildings on the farm where I grew up are now totally gone—even the magnificent barn. Most of the buildings gradually deteriorated since they were no longer needed and were finally demolished or recycled. The land on which these buildings stood is now crop land.

The small family farms of my childhood have largely disappeared. While we had a few chickens, pigs, cows, and horses, modern farmers specialize. They may raise hundreds of chickens or pigs, or a large number of beef cattle. Instead of eggs produced by free-range hens, most of the eggs we now buy at the grocery store are laid by hens cooped in narrow pens and fed a diet that maximize egg production. Milk production has moved from a few cows milked by hand to large dairies with many milk cows and modern milking machines. Some farms just specialize in raising crops—largely corn and soybeans—for the world market.

In Retrospect

Herds of livestock have grown bigger, and so have the tractors. Dad's 1939 Model B John Deere tractor had a 12 horsepower rating and weighed 3,275 pounds, or about 1.63 tons. The Model B had a two-cylinder gasoline engine. John Deere now makes a monster tractor of 629 horsepower weighing in at 27 tons, the 9629 RX. It runs on tracks and wheels and has a top speed of 25 mph. The tractor has an enclosed cab with air conditioning and heating as needed. It also sports a leather seat and an AM/FM radio. It is priced at around $575,000. In 2022 John Deere began producing a driverless tractor of some 14 tons. With 360-degree "vision" the tractor makes use of GPS technology. Because there are no other tractors, pedestrians, crosswalks, or other obstacles in the fields, a driverless tractor has an advantage over driverless cars. The tractor is designed to stop instantly if something unusual shows up in its path.

The modernization of agriculture has also impacted school systems. With fewer and smaller farm families, the country schools have long been closed and farm children bussed into towns. Four Iowa towns, including Odebolt, have consolidated into one school system. Odebolt high school—my alma mater—no longer exists as a high school and now functions as elementary and middle schools. Youth of high school age in and around Odebolt are now bussed some 20 miles to a consolidated high school. This consolidation has enabled the entire district to develop into strong educational programs.

The little Evangelical Mission Covenant Church that nurtured me has long been closed. The congregation had always been small, and when the Swedish roots were gradually diluted, the church closed. Odebolt now has two Lutheran Churches, one United Methodist, one Presbyterian, and one Catholic Church.

My immigrant parents can be counted among the many who found a new home and life in and around Iowa. While their own lives verged often on the edge of poverty, they were thankful for the opportunities offered to them. They were basically happy and grateful. My siblings and I were brought into the world and nourished by these hardworking, dedicated, and loving parents.

For that we have been endlessly grateful. My religious friends say that I have been blessed; my spiritual friends say that I have been fortunate; and my atheist friends say that I have been lucky. In retrospect, all three observations seem appropriate.

The Journey to Philosophy

My life's journey has led me through a series of vocational episodes: bridge design engineer at the Iowa Highway Commission, pastor of the Savona Federated Church in Savona, New York, and philosophy professor at Carthage College and the University of Wisconsin-Parkside. Many of my friends have asked me why I left the field of Civil Engineering and pursued other professions. My usual response is, "I became interested in problems that could not be solved with a slide-rule."

There are no doubt a number of factors that explain my journey. In high school, I enjoyed math and the sciences—such as they were in Odebolt High School. No one in my high school offered any vocational advice, and my horizons were limited. (Curiously, a Presbyterian pastor in Odebolt whom I never formally met, once asked me if I had ever considered the ministry. I had not.) Engineering appeared to be a promising field of study. My brother Howard was an engineering student at Iowa State College when I graduated from high school, so it seemed natural for me to join him at Iowa State and enroll in engineering. The curriculum was challenging, and generally satisfying. However, other interests and concerns gradually led me away from science and technology.

My own view is that the death of my father when I was thirteen years of age left a deep imprint on me. The problem of death and the various challenges that life brings to us prompt some of us to search for answers. These concerns tend to develop after the teen years. Seldom does any student enter college with the field of philosophy in mind. Philosophy majors are usually "converts." That was my story. I took my first philosophy course at Drake University one summer before my last semester at Iowa State. That course, I do believe, hooked me. I could not let go of philosophical questing. Seminary at Andover Newton Theological School, Newton Centre, Massachusetts, opened up new studies and areas of interest. And while my three years as a pastor were fulfilling in their own way, I still had a thirst for more learning. I became deeply interested in what human beings believe and why they hold the beliefs that they do. This yearning led me to graduate work at the University of Iowa. The rest, as they say, is history.

While I have ventured from that Iowa farm in many ways, those early years of love and nurturing by my parents, the little church, my country school, and my siblings have grounded me in values that I have sought to retain and practice. These values would include not only a strong moral compass, but also a respect for the dignity of common labor, persistence, patience—and a sense of humor. Another value I treasure and hope to reflect is a sense of empathy for all members of our human community as each one seeks to find a fulfilling life.

www.ingramcontent.com/pod-product-compliance
Lightning Source LLC
Chambersburg PA
CBHW051658090426
42736CB00013B/2435